PRESENTED TO:

_____

WITH LOVE FROM:

_____

ON:

_____

IF YOU THINK YOU CAN, YOU CAN!

To my kids!

Growth Mindset: It's as Easy as ABC
Copyright © 2024 by Erin Mengeu

All inquiries should be directed to www.betheirdifference.com
Paperback ISBN 979-8-9851608-3-3
Hardback ISBN 979-8-9851608-5-7
Ebook 979-8-9851608-4-0

Grab Your Free Printables by scanning this QR Code!

Published by: Be Their Difference
www.betheirdifference.com

BTD

GROWTH MINDSET

IT'S AS EASY AS ABC

WRITTEN AND ILLUSTRATED BY

Erin Mengeu

BTD

Did you know that your BRAIN is like a MUSCLE?

That's right! Your brain can grow stronger just like the muscles in your arms and legs.

Body builders lift weights to get big strong muscles.

It seems kind of silly to think of our brain lifting weights.

Even though our brain cannot really lift weights, we can still give it a GROWTH MINDSET workout!

It's as easy as ABC !

A is for ATTITUDE

ATTITUDE is how you think and feel about things.

When you have a growth mindset, it's easier to choose a positive **ATTITUDE**, even when you feel mad or sad.

Aa

B is for BELIEVE

When you **BELIEVE** in yourself, you trust yourself to make good choices and you know that you can do it.

You can do anything, if you **BELIEVE** you can!

Bb

C is for CHALLENGES

CHALLENGES make you stronger!

When you face a **CHALLENGE** and work your way through it, you learn from it, and feel great too!

Cc

D is for DIFFERENCE-MAKER

Every person can make a DIFFERENCE.

...that make the BIGGEST difference in the world!

Sometimes it is the tiniest little things

How can you be a

DIFFERENCE-MAKER?

Dd

E is for EFFORT

EFFORT is when you work really hard at something.

Taking your time, practicing, and trying new ways to get the job done are all ways to show **EFFORT**. Sometimes this feels hard, but you will be proud of your effort.

Ee

F is for FAILURES

Did you know that **FAILURES** are a good thing?

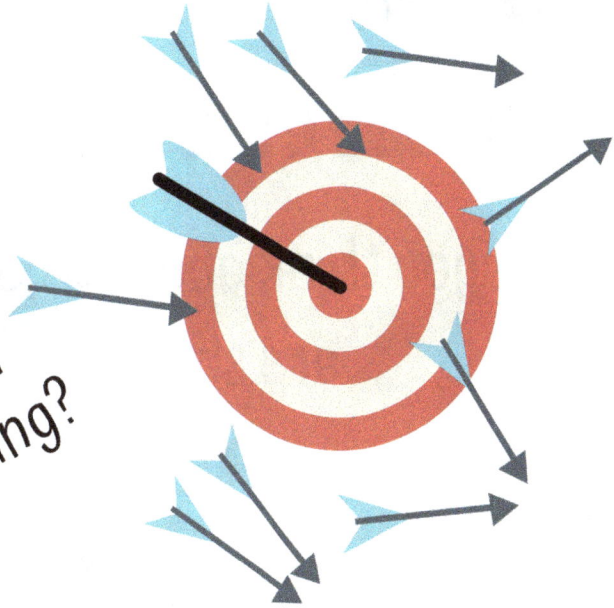

These **FAILURES** give your brain quite a workout! Each time you fail and try again, your brain learns what works and what doesn't work.

SO CELEBRATE THOSE FAILURES!

Ff

G is for GRATITUDE

When you think about what you are grateful for, you are showing GRATITUDE.

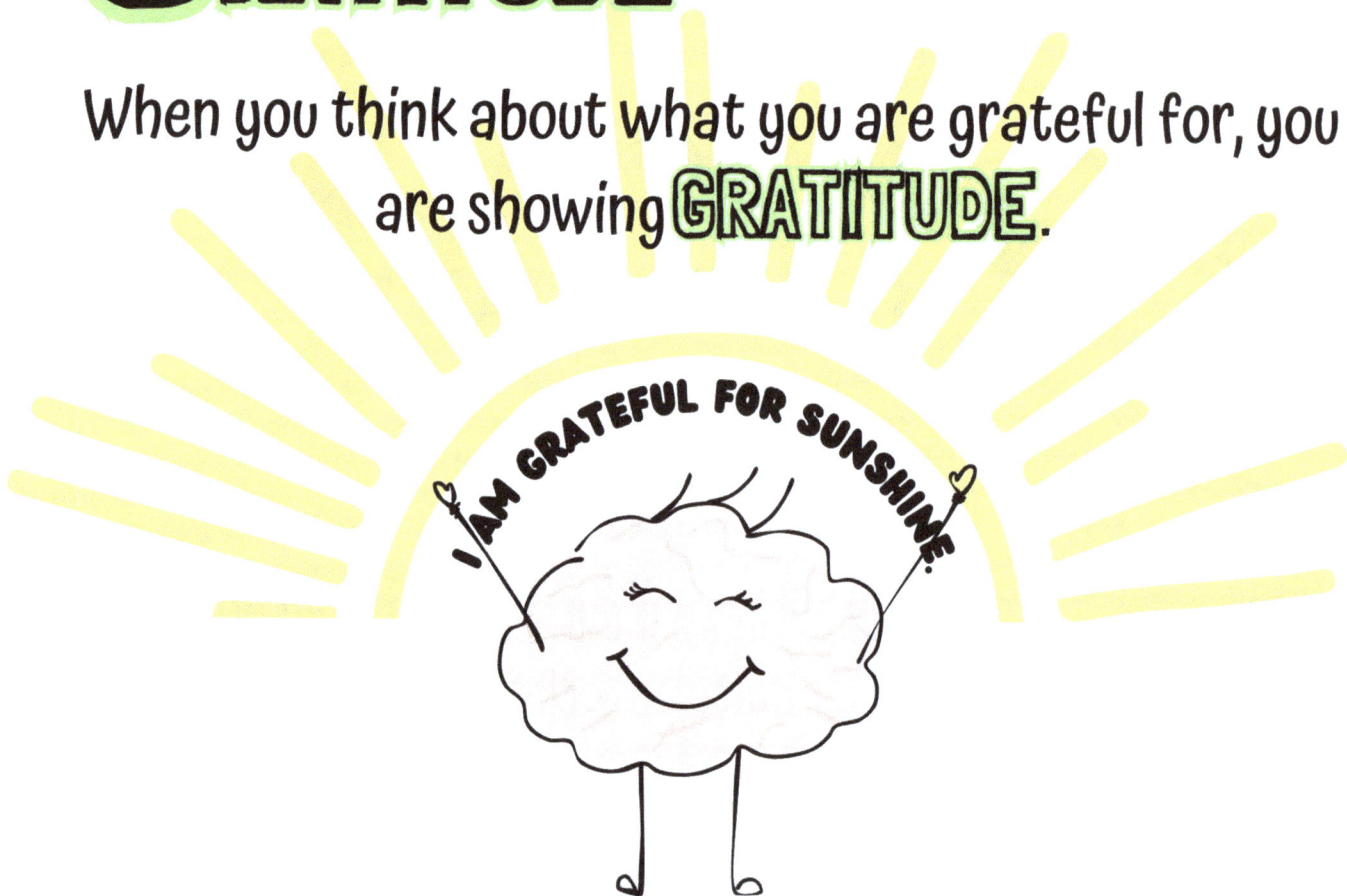

I AM GRATEFUL FOR SUNSHINE.

You can be grateful for lots of things both big and small.
Give it a try! What are you grateful for?

Gg

H is for HELP

Sometimes you will need to ask for **HELP**. Knowing when you need help and being brave enough to ask is a sign that you have a growth mindset. Most likely if you need **HELP**, chances are other people do too!

Hh

I is for IMAGINE

Being able to **IMAGINE** what you want to do or be is a great way to work your brain muscle.

You can be anything you want to be. **IMAGINE** it, work for it, and celebrate your progress every step of the way.

J is for **JOURNEY**

A **JOURNEY** is a path from one place to another.

When it comes to learning, you are on a **JOURNEY**.

You are **SMARTER TODAY** than yesterday, and you will be **EVEN SMARTER** tomorrow!

Jj

K is for KIND

Show others you care by being KIND.

Be the person that makes other people feel important.
And don't forget to be KIND to yourself.
You deserve it!

Kk

L is for LEARNING

LEARNING actually changes the shape of your brain.

Each time you work hard and practice new skills, your brain changes and you get better at what you are **LEARNING**.

Ll

M is for MISTAKES

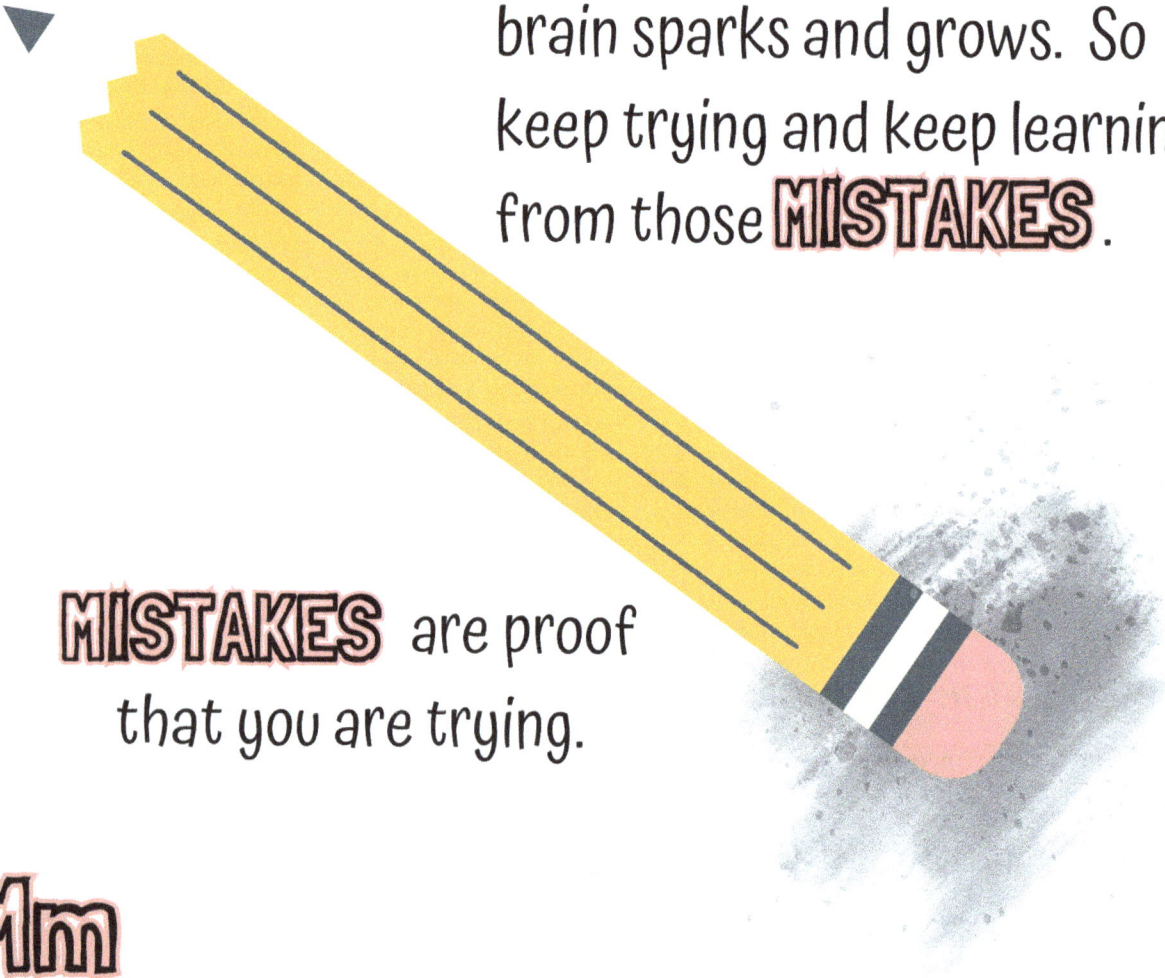

When you make a mistake your brain sparks and grows. So keep trying and keep learning from those **MISTAKES**.

MISTAKES are proof that you are trying.

Mm

N is for NOTICE

Take time to **NOTICE** what works for you and what doesn't work for you.

NOTICE WHAT WORKS!

- Practice Makes Progress
- I CAN DO IT!
- Try something new
- Think Positive
- The Power of YET
- Grateful for sunshine

When you **NOTICE** what works, stick with that and keep up the good work.

Nn

O is for OPEN-MINDED

Trying new things helps your brain grow and discover new interests.

When you are open to new ideas and ways of learning you are being OPEN-MINDED.

Oo

P is for PROGRESS

A growth mindset tells you that **PROGRESS** is more important than being perfect.

Nobody is perfect, but you can be great by making a little **PROGRESS** each day.

Pp

Q is for QUESTIONS

When you are curious or wonder about something, your brain begins to ask QUESTIONS?

Keep asking QUESTIONS and you will discover all kinds of cool things!

Qq

R is for RESILIENT

You are **RESILIENT** when you recover quickly when things get hard.

This toy bounces right back up no matter how hard we try to knock it down.

A cactus can survive in really hot and really cold weather.

Rr

S is for SUPERPOWERS

Your **SUPERPOWERS** are those special things about you that make you super! You may even have superpowers that you haven't discovered yet!

Ss

What are your **SUPERPOWERS**?

T is for THINK TIME

Give yourself and others the right amount of **THINK TIME**.

Every brain is different.

Some need more **THINK TIME** than others.
Allow time for your brain to grow and be strong.

Tt

U is for UNIQUE

BE YOU!
Be UNIQUE!

If everyone was the same, it would be so boring. Be proud of what makes you UNIQUE and you will learn to love yourself and the world around you.

Uu

V is for VISION

VISION BOARD

I will learn to tie my shoes!

Tie Shoes
Count by 5's
Read 20 min. per day

A

I am kind.
I am smart.
I can work hard.
I can take risks.

Picture the goals that you want to achieve.

When you have a **VISION**, it gives you something to strive for.

Vv

W is for WORK

Hard **WORK** is a choice.

When you decide to **WORK** hard, your brain gets a serious workout! It feels so great when you reach your goals.

Ww

X is for eXTRA

We are all a little **eXTRA** in some way.

That is what makes you who you are,
and who you are is **eXTRA**ordinary!

Xx

Z is for **ZEALOUS**

When you are really excited to learn something new and you give it all you've got, you are **ZEALOUS** for learning!

Being **ZEALOUS** for learning is proof you have a **growth mindset**!

Zz

With a growth mindset you can do anything!
Just keep giving your brain a workout, and you will see...

It's as easy as ABC!

ABCDEFGHIJKLMNOPQRSTUVWXYZ

ABOUT THE AUTHOR

Erin Mengeu, a passionate advocate for growth mindset, has witnessed firsthand the transformative power it holds. Her research on developmental growth revealed that it's never too late to reshape your brain and cultivate a growth mindset. As an adult who embraced this philosophy, Erin envisions the profound impact it could have on young learners. As a devoted mom to three energetic kids and an experienced elementary teacher with over 20 years in the field, Erin is on a mission to empower others. She believes that everyone can exercise their brain and foster a growth mindset. Now, fueled by her newfound journey, Erin is fulfilling her dream of writing a children's book. With a positive attitude and unwavering effort, she's ready to inspire young minds!

You can find Erin at **www.betheirdifference.com** where she shares effective strategies for developmental growth, resources that can be used in the classroom, and information about the graduate-level courses she teaches at the Dominican University of California.

Your voice truly matters. If you enjoyed this book, it would mean the world to me if you would leave a heartfelt review on Amazon. Your feedback is very appreciated and so very important. Thank you so much for your time.

www.ingramcontent.com/pod-product-compliance
Lightning Source LLC
Chambersburg PA
CBHW080148310326
41914CB00090B/901